Adult Coloring Book Animals of the World Volume III

Copyright © 2016

For resale and distribution information, please contact us via www.booboone.com

Male Goat

Cute Baby Deer

Common Bull by Delarno

Brown Bear by Delarno

Snow Leopard by Lena London

White-faced Capuchin Monkey

Gorilla by Delarno

Pig

Groundhog by Gennadiy Lukaynenko

Hamster by Lena London

Sloth

Rabbit by Lena London

Zebra by Lena London

Saddle Bronc Rodeo

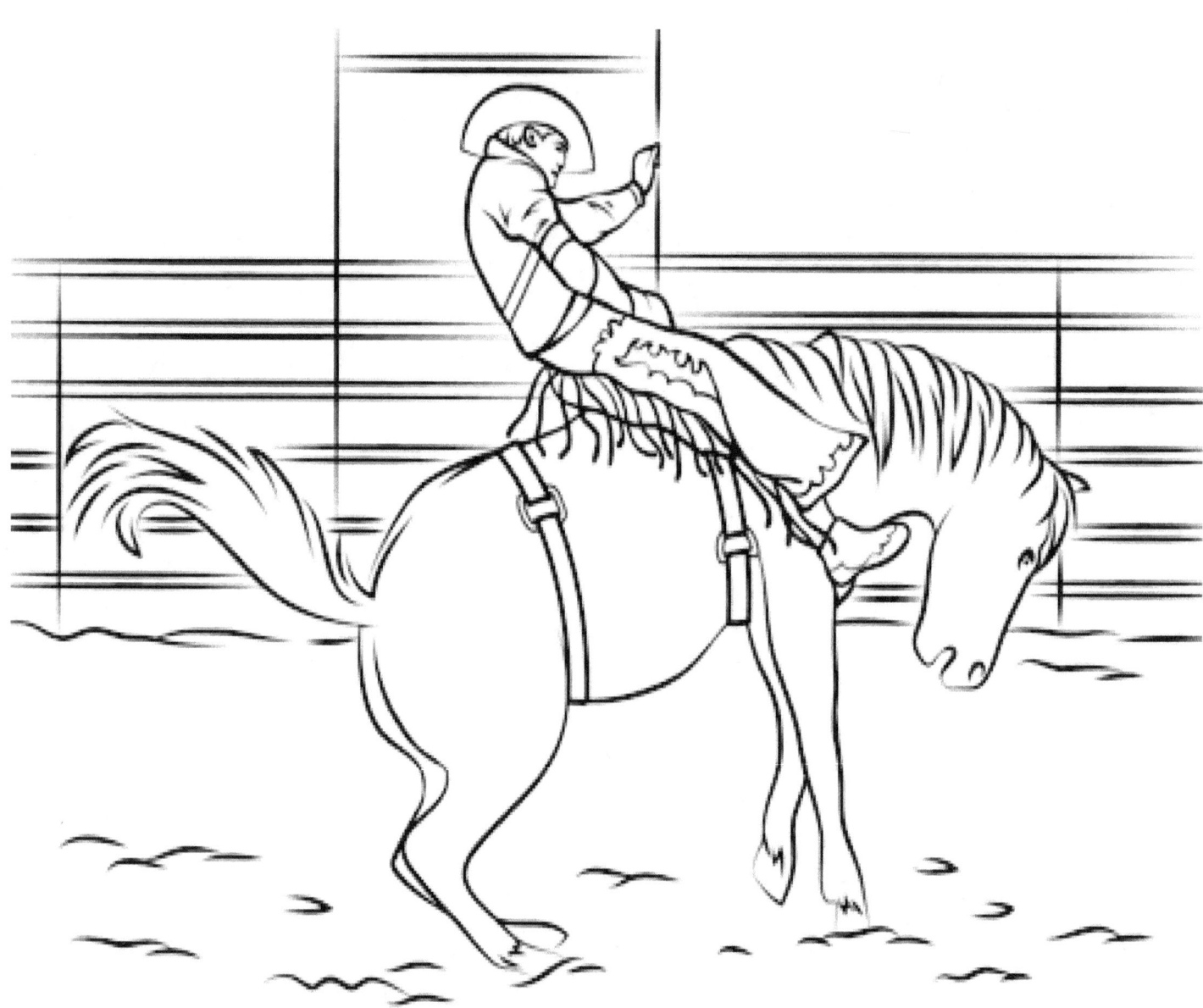

Running Horse by Lena London

Weasel

Guinea Pig Family by Gennadiy Lukaynenko

Fox

Gurnsey Cow

Horse Head

Lama by Natalia Moskovkina

Elephant

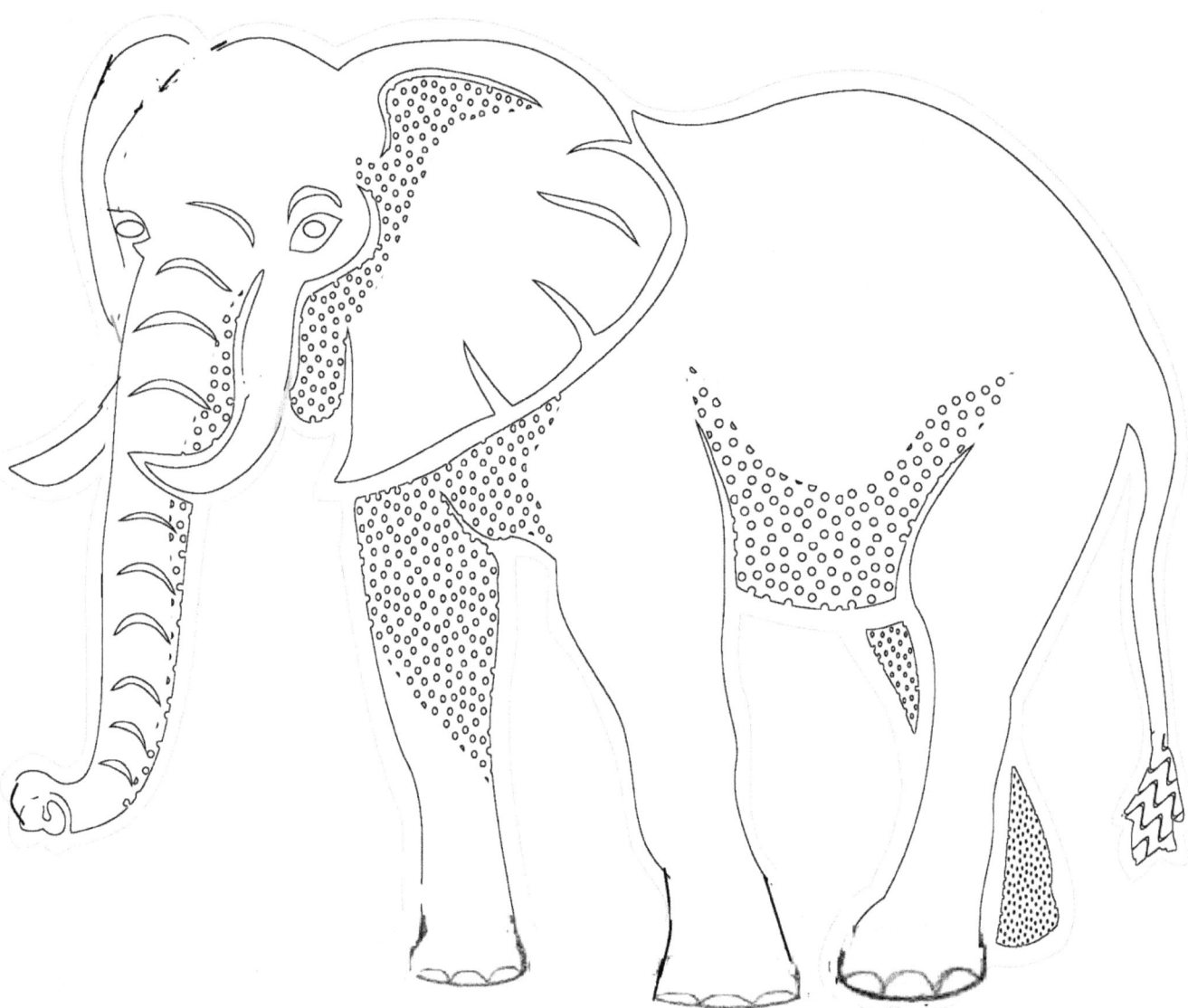

Chameleon

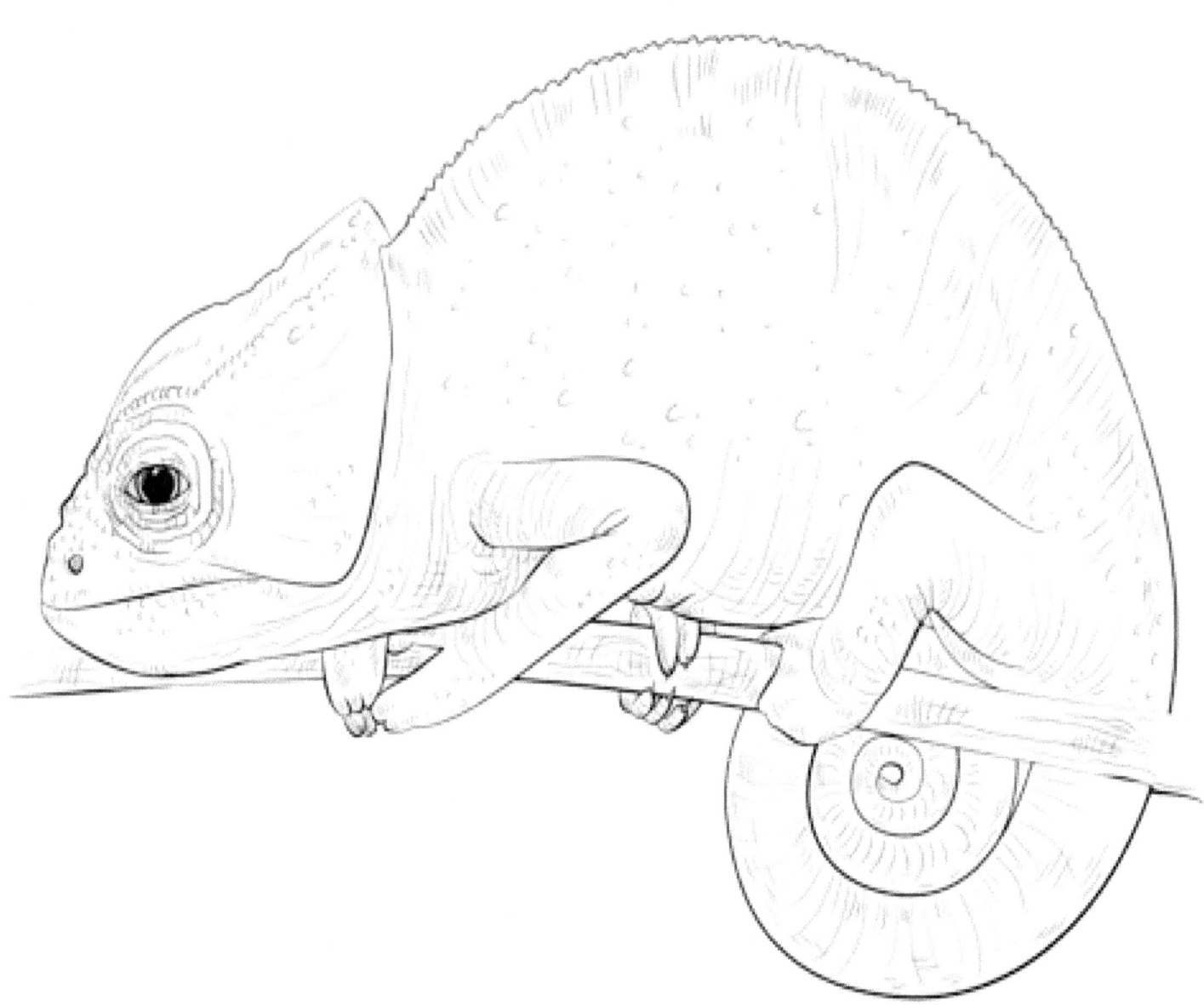

Ocelot by Lena London

Ring-tailed Lemur by Lena London

Wolf

Tasmanian Devil by Lena London

Wolverine by Lena London

Wombat

Buffalo

Eastern Chipmunk by Gennadiy Lukaynenko

Spider Monkey

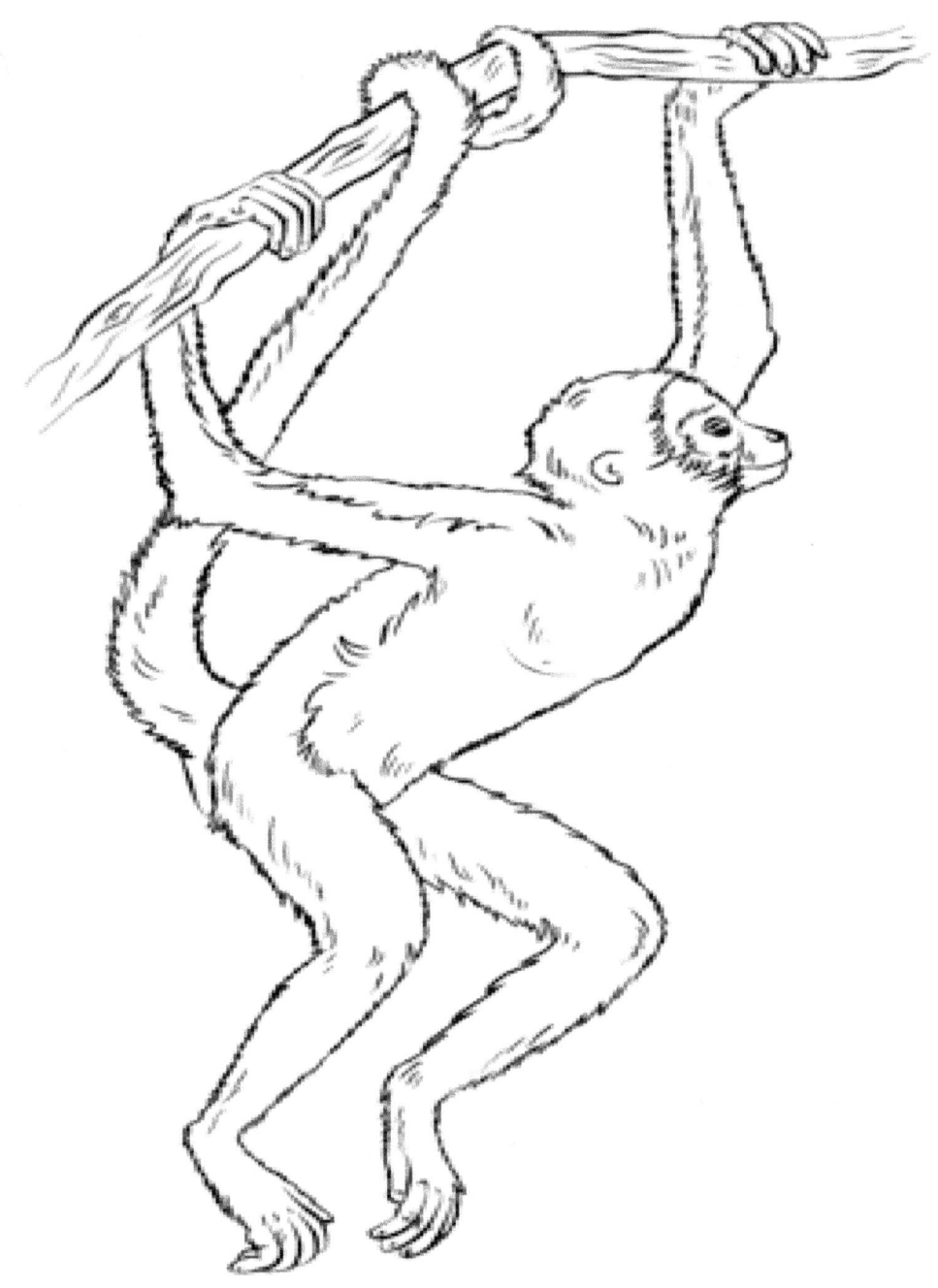

Yak by Lena London

Fawn

Female Deer by Delarno

Domestic Dog

Baby Giraffe

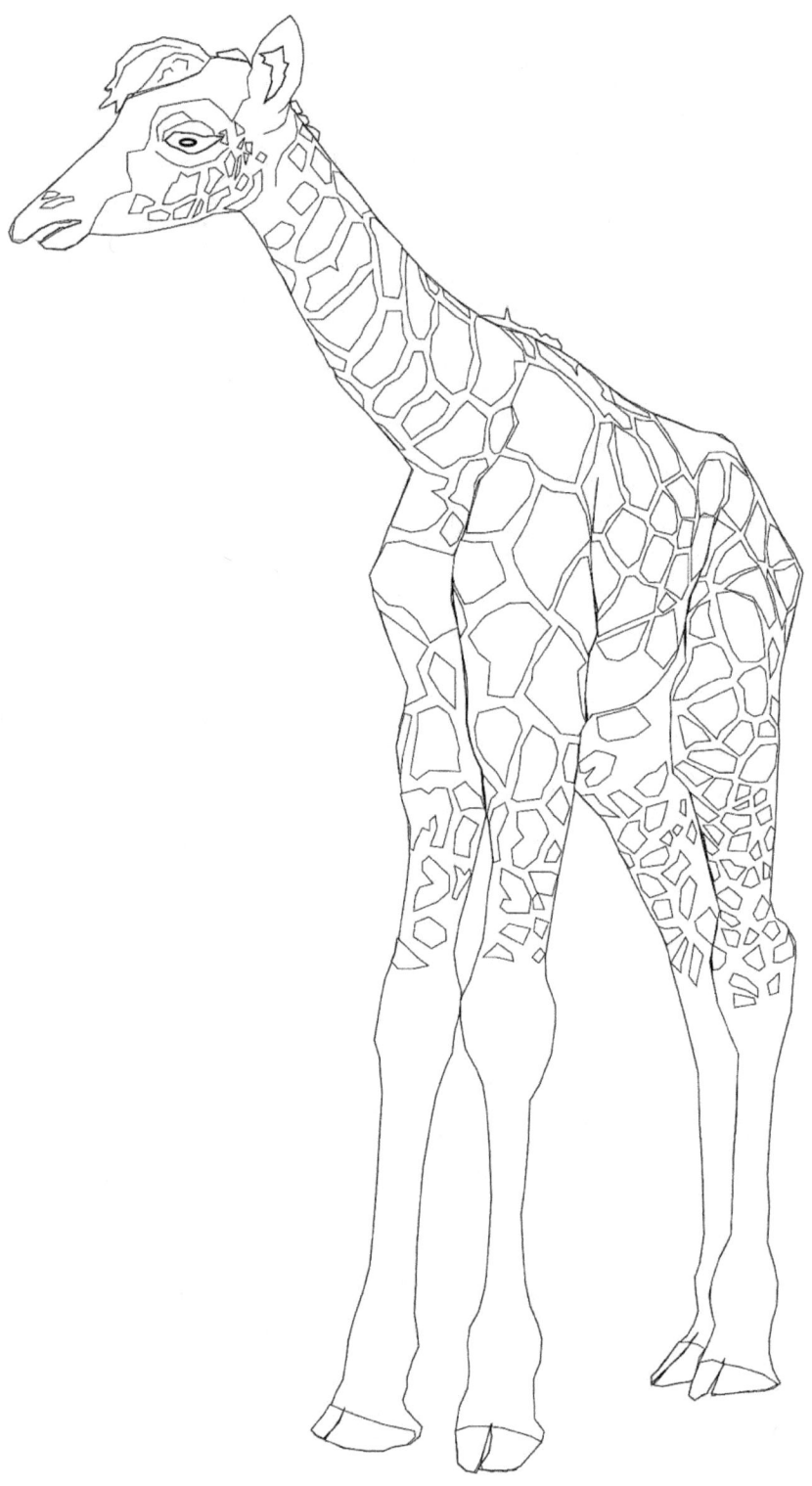

Brahma Bull

Gaur by Delarno

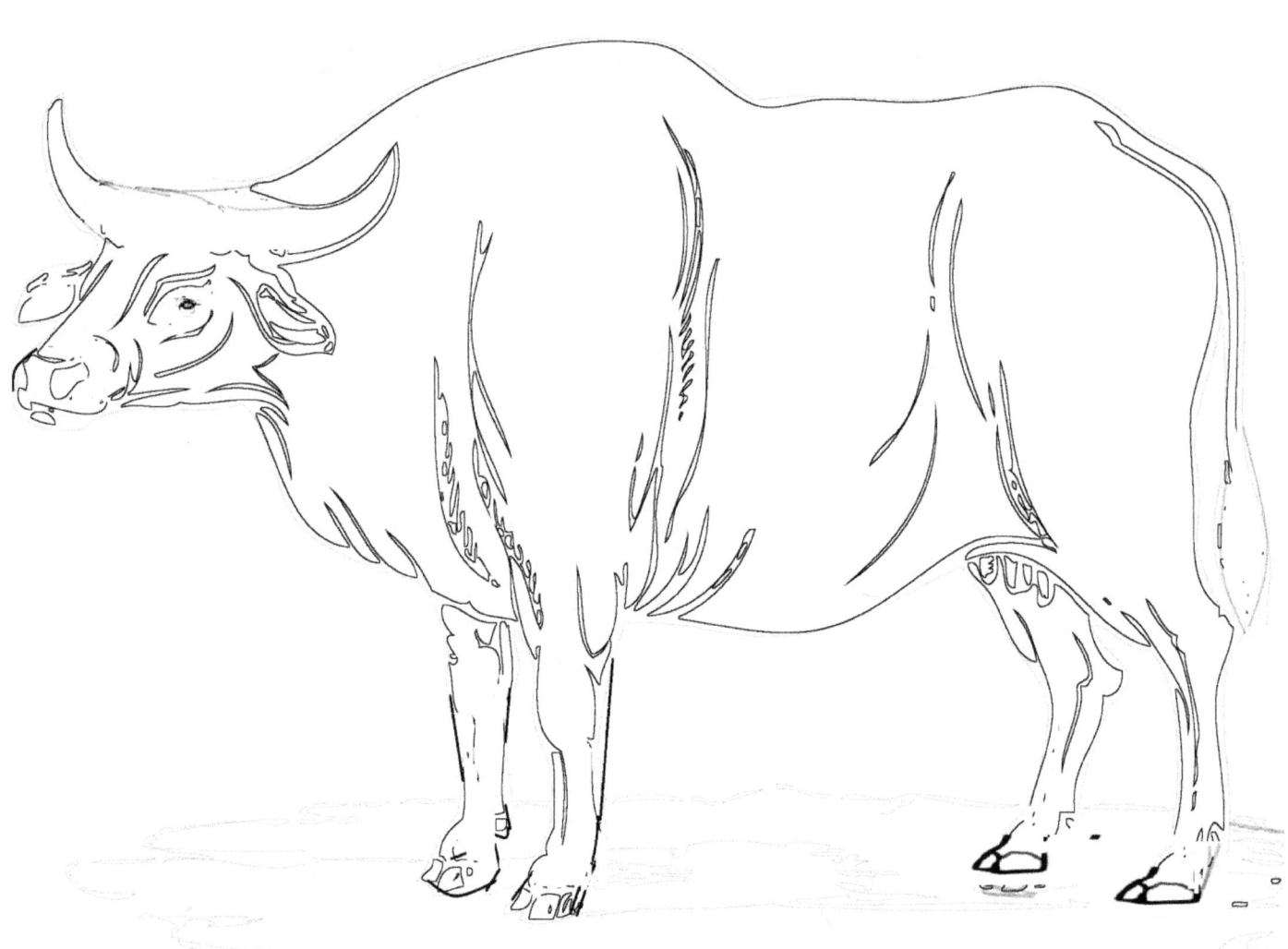

Female Goat

Panda

Mule

Young Lamb

Camel

Sika Deer

Male Giraffe

Moose

Gray Hippo

Tiger

Cute Puppy

Jackal Mother and Cub